Beginning Prayers

Compiled by

John Slow

ISBN 0 85346 199 6

© The United Reformed Church, 2000

Compiled by John Slow

Published by the United Reformed Church
86 Tavistock Place, London WC1H 9RT

Produced by Communications and Editorial, Graphics Office

Printed by Healeys Printers, Unit 10, The Sterling Complex,
Farthing Road, Ipswich, Suffolk IP1 5AP

Contents

Appreciation

Thanks are due to the wide circle of contributors whose Christian faith and down-to-earth spirituality have provided this resource for those who lead God's people into worship.

Special thanks are reserved for the people who have enabled this book to see the light of day.

Carol Rogers: who, with characteristic cheerfulness and patience encouraged the project from beginning to end.

Sara Foyle: whose imaginative flair and graphic skills designed the cover and layout.

Jane Nash: whose use of computer technology produced the first draft of the prayers, unfailingly on time.

Preface

Prayer begins with God, who takes the initiative in seeking us, surprising us, finding us and making us whole again; and then leads us to respond in wonder and mystery, praise and thanksgiving. As we pray we are drawn into the web of God's love and we are tied by its delicate threads to the whole created world.

These Beginning Prayers are taken from old and new sources. A few are written by people who have never before created a prayer.

Sometimes prayers are just what we are looking for. At other times we have to 'own' them by making our emphases, spaces for silence, possibly changing words, or better still writing our own prayers.

This book, too, needs a beginning prayer:

>Welcoming God,
>as you call us to meet you
>lead us gently
>>reverently
>>trustingly
>>sensitively
>>honestly
>>joyfully
>>imaginatively
>>creatively
>>adventurously
>>expectantly
>into your presence
>that we may worship you in spirit and in truth.

>*John Slow*
>*Ascension Day 2000*

Prayers
Before Worship

1

Living and loving God,
there are so many things we bring to you today:
the music of the organ
and our voices raised in praise;
our prayers,
silent as well as spoken,
for ourselves and for others;
the reading of the bible
and the preaching of the gospel;
the liveliness, imagination and enthusiasm
of children and young people,
and the experience of those who are older;
our gifts of flowers and money,
above all, our faith, hope and love.
Take all these things
and weave them into worship so alive
that we may become your new people,
ready to serve you in worlds of tomorrow.

2

God be in our ears
to hear the heavens telling your glory,
to be sensitive to your children gathered here,
to be aware of you in the silence,
and to hear what your voice is asking of us today.
God be in our ears
And use them for your glory.

God be in our eyes
to watch for your children,
to notice their hurts and joys,
their needs and reactions,
to laugh and cry with your people here
God be in our eyes,
And use them for your glory.

God be in our lips
to speak your word not ours,
to sing your praises and whisper your love,
to inspire and encourage,
and to kiss with your peace,
God be in our lips
And use them for your glory.

· · · · ·

. . . . .

God be in our hands
to welcome others with the squeeze
of friendship,
to share your gifts of bread and wine,
to lift others to you in prayer
and to touch with your healing love.
God be in our hands
And use them for your glory.

God be in our minds
to understand more of you,
to receive and share your wisdom,
to make connections between your kingdom and
our lives.
God be in our minds
And use them for your glory.

God be in our hearts
to open them to all your children
here today
to feel that your love is real and close,
to warm the heart of this church with your fire
to burn with your passion for all your people,
God be in our hearts
And use them for your glory.

3

Faithful, never-failing God
this is the day:

when we bring to you our praise and our prayers

when we bring our minds to seek your truth

when we bring our lives to be filled with your life

when we bring our joys .....and our sadness

when we bring our sins and ask to be forgiven and set free

This is the day you have given us
we will rejoice and celebrate

4

Loving God,
in worship
we take the risk again
of opening our lives to you.
We know
that many times before
miracles have happened;
people have discovered
you love them
forgive them
challenge them
stretch their minds
help them to grow in faith
call them to change direction
and follow you
then send them out to serve
you.
We dare to believe
it will happen again today.

We believe
help our unbelief!

Two prayers for calming nerves and hassle and over-activity ....

5

Eternal God, still us now in the silence ... *(pause)*
as we notice the sounds of nature, of traffic, of preparation,
we hear you out and about in your kingdom,
and rejoice that we are a part of it.
Our time of worship will be in your safe hands;
help us to let go and let you flow through us,
that we may draw others into the joy of your love,
through Jesus Christ our Lord.

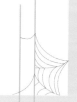

6

Lord, the time is here
and we feel unprepared and inadequate;
our worries and life's busy-ness still press in,
threatening to press you out,
our nerves threaten to distract us   *contexts*
from sensing your redeeming presence.
Welcoming God, flood us again with your love
gently lift our anxieties and fears;
remind us that we can trust you
to do with *even us* so much more than we can ask or imagine,
through Jesus Christ our Lord,
to whom be glory for ever.

On a 'bog-standard' day …! 7

Incarnate Lord,
you were born into the ordinary and everyday:
help us never to grow stale
nor take for granted the stunning grace and joy of your
presence,
help us NOW to know you
and show you,
that our worship may shine with your glory
and reveal your life-changing love,
through Jesus our Emmanuel.

*(On special occasions, when the pattern of worship is more full
and complex than usual;
when people less used to leading worship are taking part)*

Lord, we are being ambitious today;
the candles and music [*and whatever*]
and the involvement of so many people.
In all the responsibility and choreography
remind us why we are here:
to make space for the people to encounter and praise you.
In the celebration of this special occasion,
grant us the gift of sensitivity to your children
whose lives are currently dark and painful,
who find it hard to share joy.
Whoever,
whatever,
however,
help us to share your love.

To remind us of every member's ministry ....

9

Living Lord, we prepare to meet you today:
in tiny children laughing and playing;
in teenagers searching for themselves and you;
in single people sharing their lives with many as you did;
in couples and families making space in their lives for
one-another;
in the army of retired busy people, dedicated to whatever
they can do for you;
in the steadiness and experience of your oldest children,
their lasting faith in a changing world;
in the uncomfortable stranger, reminding us of your
wider world.
Lord, they are all your ministers,
may we honour and respect as we lead them,
that together we may offer true worship to the one
true God,

In times of tragedy or shock ....

10

Lord, we don't know why bad things happen,
any more than those who have gathered,
expecting us to lead them:
help us to trust you, so that our trust will show,
may we be channels of your peace,
which – especially at times like this –
the world finds hard to understand.
As you lived in the thick of this world's problems
may we not to try to be above them,
but within them
to offer gently your hope and healing love.

To acknowledge the rest of the Body of Christ in darker corners of the world ....
(This might also be a good introduction to the Lord's Prayer)

11

God of the whole world,
we meet in safety as others meet in danger and hushed
secrecy;
let us never waste our freedom to worship you.
With your gift of free speech,
let us proclaim your word confidently and clearly,
that we may encourage all your people to share you
with a too comfortable world,
a divided world,
an insecure world,
a world deaf to the cries of our brothers and sisters
who long for your kingdom of justice and joy.

12

We thank you, God,
that you have spoken to people of faith
at many times and in various ways,
and that in Jesus, your living Word,
you have revealed yourself among us.
We come longing once more to know your presence
and to hear your word.
We come eager to follow Jesus.
We rejoice that you are with us always
when we gather in his name.

13

God of all past ages,
keep us faithful to the tradition from which we grow.
God of this moment,
prepare us now to worship you in spirit and truth.
God of the future,
use this time we set aside
to draw us on towards the fulfilment of your kingdom;
through Jesus Christ, the same yesterday, today and forever.

14

Creator God,
we come to worship you;
but how can we approach the maker of heaven and earth?
Our minds are too small,
our words too feeble,
and our love too cold;
so we come in silence
simply offering
ourselves.

(silence)

we come to find ourselves in you
          to find our meaning in Jesus Christ
          to be gently inspired by the Holy Spirit
          to be re-created.

(silence)

Renew us,
refresh us,
open our minds,
widen our vision,
then we will be whole again;
and our worship
and our lives
will bring glory to your name.

15

Living God:
in this building, used to the sound of singing;
this building which has seen baptisms and funerals;
this building where people have come to be married,
or to celebrate the birth of a child;
this building where people have wept, and been filled with joy;
this building where people have wrestled with the deep things
of life,
have prayed urgently, been stirred and changed;
in this building where you have so often been with your people,
be with us now.

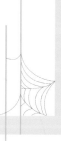

Appointment

16

Waiting God
we come
to honour our appointment
with you.
Today is your day
of new beginnings.
Today - and every day –
you offer
to initiate us
with Christ
into your Kingdom.
Wash us clean
and take away
our lovelessness,
our triviality,
our self-absorption.
Bathe us
in your nearness,
your care,
your forgiveness.
Well up in us
as a living spring:
give childlike trust,
prophetic vision
and infectious joy.
And remind us
that we have kept
this appointment with you
so that you
can appoint us.
Hold us open
to be sent
as servants and messengers
to your people
in a world
that waits
for the heavens to open
and hope to dawn.

17

Welcoming God,
in our bustle and busyness
we pause
to worship you
to be held in your eternal peace.

(silence)

Help us to get rid of all
that stands between us and you;
let us feel your warm kiss of forgiveness
let us know the gentle embrace of acceptance.

(silence)

In the silence of eternity
you spoke and the universe was created;
in the silence of the garden
you spoke to Adam;
in the silence of the tomb
you wrought the resurrection of Jesus;
in the silence of 'now'
make us new.

18

Living God,
we meet together
to celebrate your love
and to share your Word.

Speak and help us to listen,
listen and help us to speak,
that in praise
prayer
and preaching
you may touch our lives
and make us whole again.

19

Lord, set your blessing on us
as we begin this day together.
Confirm in us the truth
by which we rightly live;
confront us with the truth
from which we wrongly turn.
We ask not for what we want
but for what you know we need,
as we offer this day and ourselves
for you and to you;
through Jesus Christ our Saviour.

20

You are here, Jesus
welcoming us with your open arms

You are here, Jesus
encircling us with your love

You are here, Jesus
reaching out to touch us with healing,
making us whole

You are here, Jesus
stilling the storms within us and around us
with your 'Peace, be still'

You are here, Jesus
waiting to refresh us with your Word

You are here, Jesus
loosening our tongues to praise you

You are here, Jesus
calling us to serve you

You are here, Jesus
speaking words of comfort and assurance
'Your sins are forgiven, go in peace'

Thanks be to God!

21

Thank-you God
for your Church
for our church,
for the one-anotherness that exists between us,
encouragement we receive
when we doubt ourselves
or when things could go better,
joy shared in our celebrations,
concern and care shown when we are ill,
small kindnessess worth much more than their value,
signs of your Spirit's work among us.

Flood our lives with your love today
so that it will overflow
into the lives of those around us.

22

Lord, we come again into your house
a protected environment
where we can be still in your presence,
fed and watered by your Word,
comforted and reassured by your warmth and light.

We cannot stay in our 'greenhouse',
like plants we will never grow strong
unless we experience the movement
and buffeting
of the wind of your Spirit
encouraging our roots to go deeper,
secure in your love.

Holy Spirit, move among us
enable us to understand your Word and its relevance for
our lives
so that individually and as a church
we will grow closer to what you would have us be.

For the day when our world seems to be falling apart

23

Listening God,
out of the depths we cry to you,
the depths of our grief, our anger,
our confusion, our unanswered questions,
our feelings of guilt,
our unfulfilled dreams, our shattered hopes;
perhaps all that we bring to you today
is a jumble of broken pieces
and we want to be made whole again.

Help us to open ourselves to your presence
    our minds to your truth
    our hearts to your love
    our spirits to your healing.

24

Living, loving God,
in the name of your dear Son, Jesus Christ,
we meet together today
in this special place
to worship you.

Take your people here
lift up their hearts,
encourage their souls,
enliven their minds,
that together we might be
a people of worship, praise, thanksgiving and renewal,
a people you call by name and know,
a people who long for healing and wholeness,
with your life in theirs.

Bless with all the gifts and graces of your Spirit
those who will lead, serve, sing, pray,
read and preach your word.
May all we do in this place
help us to know ourselves to be your people,
bearing witness to your glory in our lives,
for the advancement of your kingdom
and the sake of your Son,
Jesus Christ our Lord.

25

Almighty God, our Father
help us to worship you sincerely,
to listen to you attentively,
and to respond to the teaching of your Spirit.
Bless those appointed to special responsibilities
in the service,
and ourselves as we share in it
for the glory of Jesus Christ our Lord.

A Prayer for Stillness

26

God of stillness and creative action
help us to find space in the quietness today,
that we may live creatively,
discover the inner meaning of silence
and learn the wisdom that heals the world.
Send peace and joy to each quiet place,
to all who are waiting and listening.
May your still small voice be heard
through Jesus Christ in the love of the Spirit.

27

In a world vibrating with action
we have come here to be still.

In a world of tight schedules and deadlines
we have come to absorb the present.

In a world of limits and frustrations
we have come to the brink of eternity.

At the still point of our churning world
we can meet the unchanging God
and know his peace.

Prayers
at Beginning
of Worship

28

God the Creator,
you have given to us the task of being creators;
with the beauty of this building we worship you,
in brick and stone,
glass and wood,
in design and shape;
colour and texture.

God the Saviour,
you have come to us in Jesus;
in our daily discipleship we worship you,
in prayer and praise,
word and work,
tears and laughter.

God the life-giving Spirit,
you bind us together in the life of the Church;
in our experience of unity we worship you;
with faith and love,
hope and vision,
joy and commitment.

29

God, you make all things new;
every dawning you re-create the world.
We rejoice in the freshness of today.

God, you come to us in Jesus,
your first and last word;
whenever we gather in his name
you are there among us.
We rejoice in your presence this morning.

God, you hold us together in the fellowship of the Spirit,
you inspire, strengthen, challenge and disturb us.
**We rejoice that in our worship
you will move among us now.**

30

For the gifts of joy and hope and love
which this day brings
may Jesus Christ be praised

For being there in the light
when it is so easy to believe
may Jesus Christ be praised

For being there in the darkness
when our faith is stretched to breaking point
may Jesus Christ be praised

For the fellowship of the church
which encircles us, holds us, makes us strong
may Jesus Christ be praised

For making God real to us,
and credible
may Jesus Christ be praised

For reaching out to touch our lives in worship
may Jesus Christ be praised

31

Gracious God, we greet you

This day you have given us.

Loving God, we meet you

As our voices rise in praise.

Caring God, we entreat you

Through word and song and prayer:

Be with us on our journey

in the way that lies ahead.

Reading: I Peter 2. vv.9-10

32

Let us sing praises to God
    for he has come into our life
    like a shaft of sunlight
    calling us out of the shadows
    where we were hiding,
    summoning us to praise and to service
    as a rejoicing community.

Let us sing praises to God
    for he has given us all the delight
    of worship and of ministry,
    of compassion and of care,
    as citizens of a new kingdom,
    so that all priestly barriers are shattered
    in the servant ministry of a united people.

Let us sing praises to God
    for he has equipped us by his Spirit,
    with gifts of goodness and openness,
        gifts of humility and optimism,
        gifts of healing and comfort,
        gifts of wisdom and hope.

Let us sing praises to God
    for he has achieved great wonders
    through people who have listened and obeyed;
    he has displayed the futility of selfishness
    and the folly of violence;
    he has proclaimed the eternal victory
    of a people who seek peace, joy and love
    according to the way of Jesus Christ.

33

We are thankful
that we have been led to worship you.
This is central in our lives,
leading us towards your purposes
and your love.
We rejoice to be with your people
gathered for worship;
from this we receive encouragement.

So we pray for all who are with us in this moment;
those who sit beside us;
those in the circle of faith whom we know;
those whose prayers are joined with ours.

May we know
the spirit that makes us one
and the truth that makes us free,
so that our worship
may be a part of your life,
O God our Creator and our End.

34

**May our eyes be open to see God
our minds receptive to God
our ears ready to listen to God.**

May we take the mystery
and the reality
of God's presence
with us into our daily living
that even in our weakness
his glory may be shown.

35

Praise to God for the gifts of the past:
for the witness of the people of God who went before us.

Praise to God for the gifts of the present:
we meet Christ and serve him in friend and stranger.

Praise to God for the gifts of the future:
in darkness and in light the Spirit will lead us.

Leader:	God of life of all life and of each life we lay our lives before you. We open our lives to you, from whom nothing in us is hidden.	*36*

Men   *You are before us, Lord, you are behind;*

Women   *You are in the light and in the darkness;*

Men   *You see our most public face;*

Women   *You know the secret thoughts of every heart.*

Men   *We bring the faith that is in us, and the doubt;*

Women   *We bring the joy that is in us and the sorrow;*

Men   *We bring the pride that is in us, and the shame;*

Women   *We bring the knowledge that is in us, and the*
                          ignorance;

Men   *We bring the hope that is in us and the despair;*

Women   *We bring the courage that is in us and the fear;*

Leader   God give us grace to walk in the way of Christ.

All   *Guide us by your Spirit,*
              strengthen us against all evil.
              In Jesus' name. Amen.

Before Bible Study

37

We come
to sit at the feet
of Jesus:
**as the people
did in Galilee.**

We come
to listen
to his word:
**help us to listen
and understand.**

We come
to be challenged
by the stories
told long ago:
**make them real
to us now.**

Jesus
spoke of seeds
which fell on
different soils,
and of those
which fell on good soil
and grew strong:
**plant the seed
of your purpose
in us today;
give us strength
to grow in faith,
and wisdom
to proclaim it
in all we do.**

We come into the presence
of our God
to worship and praise him.

Before Communion

38

Loving God,
when we break bread with thanksgiving
may the presence of Jesus be with us.
When we recall his words
may we be taught by you.
When we hymn your praise
may we catch the echo of the saints who sing for ever.

Before Communion, especially with children present and sharing

39

We are here
because Jesus has invited us.

When Jesus was on earth,
he often enjoyed
meals with his friends.

On the night before he died,
when darkness was beginning to fall,
he sat at table with the disciples
in an upper room in Jerusalem.

At this Last Supper,
he broke the bread and took wine,
and told his disciples
to remember him
by following his example.

Today, we are his disciples,
and we are glad to do what he has told us.

Prayers before the reading of Scripture and/or sermon

40

Living God,
may your Word come alive among us
that we may hear again the call of Christ
and then go forward to serve him
in the power of the Spirit.

41

Inspiring God,
as you touch our minds and hearts
may we wrestle with the words of Scripture
until we discover your Word for us,
then help us to make the vital connections
between the Word and the world
for your glory's sake.

42

Speak, Lord to our speaking
Speak, Lord to our thinking
Speak, Lord to our souls' deep understanding

Before Leaving Worship

43

Gracious God,
for your love for us,
gentle as a shower,
healing our pain,
binding up our wounds,
we give you thanks.

For your love for us,
sure as the dawn,
transforming our darkness,
revealing your truth,
we give you thanks.

For your love for us,
mercifully steadfast,
calling us to you,
raising us up,
we give you thanks.

For your love for us,
encouraging questions,
open to our doubts,
making us vulnerable,
we give you thanks.

For your steadfast love
has brought us to faith.
Your steadfast love
has cradled a new creation.
Your reconciling power
has brought to birth
a new ministry.
> Urge us on, O Christ,
> to find wholeness
> through serving you
> by serving others,
> in the power of the Spirit.

Before Leaving Worship

44

Every day,
living God,
every day I will wake
to speak of you;
not in choice language
and perfect paragraphs
but in the way I expect your surprises,
    in the delight I take in sharing
        your healing moments,
    in the determination you give me
        to be a refuge for the battered and bruised,
            a rock for the tossed and troubled,
            a harbour for the grieving and angry.

Every day
I will seek to be a witness for you
    not through articulate testimony
    or a vast wardrobe of texts
but through the brightness of my face
    when pain is all I feel inside
and through the hope my eyes disclose
    as I share another's sadness.

Every day
I will proclaim the miracle of your love
not limited by narrow horizons
    of church, nation and self
but breathing the pure open air of your Spirit
    by which the light of the nations can shine
    and all be reconciled to you in Jesus Christ.

Every day
I will rejoice and be glad for all
who knowing you as loving Lord
    draw the world's attention
    not to themselves
    but to Jesus Christ
who alone deserves the glory
for ever and ever.

Before a Retreat or Quiet Day

45

Seeking God,
in the quietness
you will come very close to us;
this is the place
and the time
when our lives may be turned upside down.

While we are still,
feelings
thoughts
and memories
will float to the surface
from the deep within us.

While we are silent
you will speak,
and clearly
or hazily
we shall recognise your voice.

So we walk with you
into the unknown.

At the beginning of a new day

46

Lord, at the dawning of each new day,
you offer a fresh beginning.
Thank you for the ways by which you bless your world,
and for your presence in each situation.
May I use every opportunity to help others
to encounter Christ at their point of need (*Silence*).
And may what I say, share and do be to your glory.

At the beginning of a Church Meeting

47

God of Jubilee,
we turn to you for the life of the churches;
where there is generosity in us,
expand it with your grace;
where our longing for newness has run dry,
refresh it with your truth;
where there is creativity of heart,
deepen it with your wisdom;
where there is hope of reconciliation,
add your power to make us one.
Give us honesty of mind,
passion for justice,
and courage to choose your prophetic way.

Turn your face to us in grace, O God
and breathe into us the life of your Spirit.

At the beginning of a Church Meeting

48

Calling and sending God,
create in each of us and all of us
a clear sense of vocation,
that we may be a missionary congregation,
rejoicing together in the variety of gifts
you have planted in us –
that the world may believe.

At the beginning of a Church Meeting

49

Lord of the church,
    enable your people to be the Church:
    a redeemed people;
    a united people;
    a missionary people;
    and, in all things,
    a people gladly submissive to the truth
    as it comes to us in Jesus,
    in whose name we pray.

At the beginning of a Church Meeting

50

Persuasive God
calling us from the familiar
into territory strange and new.
daring travel
from assenting and knowing
into questioning uncertainty –
teach us how to live by faith.

Leading God,
guiding us from the accustomed
into untried, untested ways,
beckoning us
from tradition and culture
into search and adventure –
teach us how to live by faith.

Caring God,
wooing us from the conventional
into your freedom and life,
transforming us
from fear and reluctance
into love's boldness and joy –
teach us how to live by faith.

Gracious God, as we share our experience of your
presence with each other, we celebrate those people,
places and events which witness to your glory.
Help us to give thanks for the gifts you have given us.
Grant to us – a small part of your Church worldwide –
a vision of your purpose for the Church in our day.
Enable us through loving service and faithful witness
to play our part in your saving plan for the world.
This prayer we offer to you in the name of Jesus Christ,
Amen

At the beginning of a Church Meeting

Reading: Hebrews 11 v 32 – 12 v 3

51

God,
as we deal with the business before us
remind us of your unchanging call
to follow Jesus
and to be his people in the world,
lest we forget it
ignore it
evade it
reject it
or deny it.
It is so easy for the church
to depart from its faith
to be governed by fear instead of love
to become caught up
in its own interests
pettiness
conflicts
survival
even to worship other gods.

Help us to keep our eyes fixed on Jesus
on whom faith depends from start to finish.

At the beginning of a Church Meeting

Reading: Ephesians 1 vv 3-14

52

Creating God,
you paint on a vast canvas
and your greatness leaves us lost for words.
You chose us
from the beginning,
to share in your plan,
to bring all creation together
with Christ as head,
and your grace goes far beyond our deserving.
Enlarge our vision
as we search
and sometimes struggle
to discover your will for us;
enable us to see our discussions and decisions
as part of your eternal purpose;
and to you be praise and glory for ever.

At the beginning of a Church Meeting

53

Calling God,
it has been a rush to get here
and our minds are so active,
mulling over things said and done today,
planning for tomorrow.
Still us now,
set our minds
and hearts
on the business ahead;
but may this be more than just another meeting.
Help us
to seek your will
rather than follow our own agenda;
to reflect on what our faith says about our decisions,
rather than getting through the business
as quickly as possible;
to spend time on the issues that matter
rather than on our soapbox;
to be open to new possibilities
rather than closed to any change;
to remember, above all, that we are here
to discover the mind of Christ.

Prayers for the Christian Year and Special Occasions

Advent

54

Worship and praise belong to you, God our maker.
Out of nothing, you called all worlds to be,
and still you draw the universe to its fulfilment.
Dawn and evening celebrate your glory
till time shall be no more.

In Christ your Son
the life of heaven and earth were joined,
sealing the promise of a new creation
given, yet still to come.

Taught by your Spirit,
we who bear your threefold likeness
look for the City of Peace
in whose light we are transfigured
and the earth transformed.

Advent

55

Advent God,
keep us
from hurrying towards Christmas
lest we reach it too soon
and miss some of its wonder and mystery.

May we wait with patience
while you prepare us
to celebrate the festival.

May we watch for your surprises as
unannounced
and incognito,
you come into our lives each day.

Christmas

56

Jesus, people celebrate your birth in different ways.
For some, the festival means no more than
eating, drinking and making merry.
They are not likely to feel concern
about the other half of the world
which is hungry today
and will be hungry again tomorrow.

Other people enjoy the religious flavour of Christmas.
They sing carols
and listen to stories
of shepherds and angels,
a star and a stable,
Mary and Joseph and their baby lying in a manger.

But deep beneath are the greatest themes:
glory to God,
peace on earth,
good news,
great joy,
the Word made flesh.

Jesus, as we prepare to celebrate your coming amongst us,
help us to understand more of your love for all people
and to see what you are doing now in the world
that we may be caught up in your great purpose
for the whole of creation.

Christmas

Welcome Jesus,
God-with-us
in a lonely world
>Let your presence convince us
>that as years come and go
>nothing in all creation
>can separate us from your love.

Welcome Jesus,
stable child
in an unstable world.
>Let your human weakness
>fill us with amazement
>as we discover the risk you took
>to be with us.

Welcome Jesus,
fragile child
in a violent world.
>Let Herod's tantrums be exposed
>as futile and pointless
>for God's weakness
>is stronger than human anger.

Welcome Jesus,
gracious child
in a merciless world.
>Let your forgiveness
>give us God's clue
>to healing
>and securing permanent relationships.

>>Come with us Jesus
>>into another year.
>>Pitch your tent
>>and stay.

57

Christmas

58

Jesus
gift of God
to a worn-out world,
    let your presence
    open our eyes
    to see your salvation.

        Jesus
        gift of God
        to a violent world,
            let your presence
            guide our feet
            into the way of peace.

Jesus
gift of God
to an unprepared world,
    let your presence
    rouse our sleeping spirits
    into welcome and worship.

        Jesus
        gift of God
        to a rebellious world,
            let your presence
            confront our disobedience,
            redirecting our lives
            and transforming our society.

Jesus
Christmas gift
to us and the world,
    we offer you our lives
    that they in turn
    may be a gift to your world
    for its peace, its joy, its future
    displaying for all time
    your self-emptying pilgrimage to power and glory.

Christmas

59

How small Christmas is –

    a tiny baby
    in a wooden manger
    in an insignificant town

How huge Christmas is –

    the eternal God
    in wondrous love
    embraces and saves the world

Thanks be to God for his gift beyond words!

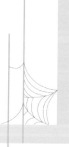

New Year

60

Jesus, the light
came
and scattered the darkness;
a child in a manger gave hope to a broken world.

Jesus, the light
will come
in the dawning of a new year.

**The light shines in the darkness
and the darkness has never put it out.**

New Year

61

Lord of the ages,
you are our beginning and our end.
Everlasting God, we place our days within your care.
Eternal Father, we trust you.
For your faithfulness in the past, we thank you;
for your constant care we praise you;
for our future in your love, we place ourselves
into your keeping and offer our lives for your service;
through Jesus Christ, your eternal Son,
our Saviour.

Epiphany

62

Worship and praise belong to you, Father,
in every place and at all times.
You made us,
and all the peoples of the world,
and everything that is.

You give us the daylight.
Your Word lights up our minds.
Jesus was born among us
to be light in our darkness.

Your Spirit lives in us
so that we can look at the world with your eyes.

Lent

Lenten Journeys

63

> Christ of the desert,
> We will walk with you
> through darkness
>> testing
>> doubt
>> disappointment
>> failure
>> betrayal
>> loneliness
>> desolation
>> suffering
>> death
> on your road to Resurrection.
>
> And you will walk with us
> in the wilderness of this world
> through darkness
>> testing
>> doubt
>> disappointment
>> failure
>> betrayal
>> loneliness
>> desolation
>> suffering
>> death
> on our road to Resurrection.

Lent

64

20/3/11

Lord Jesus Christ,
you called your disciples to go forward with you
on the way to the cross.
Since you first walked that road
countless millions have followed you.
In all that we do as your disciples,
save us from false familiarity with your journey.
May we never presume to step into your shoes,
but make us small enough to fit our own,
and to walk in love and wonder behind you.

Palm Sunday and Holy Week

Jesus, we stand before you.

We stand with the great crowd at the festival,
we shout hosanna
and praise you as the coming king,
the answer to our dreams.

We stand with Judas in the garden,
siding with the police and the chief priests,
selling out to power and money,
betraying you to violence.

We stand with Peter, trying to be loyal,
but getting it wrong, not ready for defeat,
fighting back with bloodshed and deceit,
though you must drink the cup and die.

We stand with Pilate in the praetorium,
trying to escape the choice between good and bad,
shuttling between diplomacy and truth,
abdicating to a crowd.

We stand with soldiers to mock and gamble round the cross,
following instructions,
and looking to ourselves
while you look down on us as king.

We stand with Mary, pierced by grief,
but finding at the cross
the love that had seemed lost
and the beginning of our faith.

As Easter people,
we cannot pretend
that you are not risen,
but today we stand within the shadow of your cross.

Jesus, we stand before you.

65

Palm Sunday and Holy Week

66

Lord Jesus Christ,
in this sacred and solemn week
when we see again the depth and mystery
of your redeeming love,
help us
to follow where you go,
to stop where you stumble,
to listen when you cry,
to hurt as you suffer,
to bow our heads in sorrow when you die,
so that when you are raised to life again
we may share your endless joy.

Good Friday

67

It is finished, Lord.
Your voice is now silent,
the voice which brought healing and hope,
called unlikely fishermen
and a tax collector
to follow you,
challenged people to turn their lives in a new direction.

Christ of the cross
Now you leave the work to us.

It is finished, Lord.
Your eyes are now closed,
the eyes which saw the lostness of people,
like sheep without a shepherd;
and the possibilities within people
to make your kingdom come alive.

Christ of the cross
Now you leave the work to us.

It is finished, Lord.
Your ears are now deaf,
the ears which listened
joyfully to children,
patiently to disciples who argued about
who should have the best seats in your kingdom,
lovingly to those who came to you at their wits' end.

Christ of the cross
Now you leave the work to us.

. . . . .

. . . . .

It is finished, Lord.
Your hands are now still,
the hands which cooled the fever,
touched the leper,
broke the bread and shared it,
and, reaching out to the whole world,
were nailed to the cross,
'the most accurate picture of God the world has ever seen.' *

Christ of the cross
Now you leave the work to us.

As we enter the darkness of tonight and tomorrow,
help us to wait trustingly,
expectantly,
ready to greet you,
and to be surprised by you,
our risen Lord,
on Easter morning.

**Then, in the power of your resurrection,
send us on our way
to do the work you have left us.**

* *These words come from a memorable sentence
in 'The Foolishness of God' by John Austin
Baker: 'The crucified Jesus is the only accurate
picture of God the world has ever seen, and
the hands that hold us in existence are pierced
with unimaginable nails.' (p.406)*

Easter

68

Father
sometimes
I think
that
Easter
was something
that happened
only to Jesus
a long time ago
because
he had been so good
and perfect
but then
it dawns on me
that
Easter
is a gift
which
you give away
to your world
so that
people
of all nations
can be reborn
and I
this very day
can come back to life
to serve you
in love
and hope.

Easter

69

We know that Jesus is alive,
not only from reading the story in the gospels,
nor just by being nurtured in the Church's faith,
but because we have met him.
We made the discovery once,
perhaps more than once,
that Jesus is alive for us,
and for our world.

The risen Jesus showed us the truth,
simple, yet profound,
that without the pain of dying, there is no Resurrection
without the dying .... no Resurrection.

So help us, Lord, to live Resurrection;
within ourselves
finding opportunity in disappointment,
peace in pain,
faith in doubt.

Lord, help us to share Resurrection;
in the family of the Church,
loving one another,
accepting one another,
forgiving one another,
bearing one another's burdens.

Lord, help us to proclaim Resurrection;
within the human family,
celebrating Christ's life which has conquered death
and his love which has scattered the powers of evil.

'Praise be to the God and Father of our Lord Jesus Christ,
who in his great mercy gave us new birth into a living hope
by the resurrection of Jesus Christ from the dead!.'

Easter

70

We thank you God for this amazing day,
when our hearts dance like the shining sun,
when all the world leaps with life
and the great, infinite wonders of the earth
shout their 'yes!' to you.

We who have seen death,
who have heard the story of the cross
and sorrowed deep at the sharp agony of the world's pain,
we have come to life again
in the life of your Son.

With Christ we have been lifted from the nothing of death
into your new and unimagined life,
where tasting, touching, hearing, seeing and breathing,
are more sweet than we had known before
and where you are in beauty and in truth.
How could we ever doubt you,
when today your Spirit makes us want to dance and shout,
to the praise of the risen one,
the one who has defeated death and all the evil powers?
How could we ever doubt you,
now that our ears are awake and our eyes are opened?

We thank you God for this amazing day,
when the evil in us lies down dead,
and the good in us is born again.
This is the birth day of life and love and goodness.
This is the amazing day,
when our Saviour rose, when the earth released him,
when the heavens echoed the praise of earth, on this great day.
Alleluia! to out leaping, rising, lively, infinite, God.

This prayer was inspired by the reading from John's
Gospel and by a sonnet by e e cummings: I thank you
God for most this amazing day.

Ascension

71

Jesus Christ is Lord

This is *our confession of faith*:
made in distinctive commitment
to walk in the way of Jesus.

Jesus Christ is Lord

This is *our statement of belief*:
hammered out and continually re-shaped by the truth
at the blurred edges of the Church and the world.

Jesus Christ is Lord

This is *our experience of unity*:
shared with fellow-pilgrims on the journey.

Jesus Christ is Lord

This is *our political manifesto*:
challenged to live by the values of God's upside-down
kingdom.

Jesus Christ is Lord

This is *our call to evangelism*:
to tell God's story
and to invite others to take the first risky steps
in the dance of faith.

Jesus Christ is Lord

**This is the heart of our celebration.
Alleluia!**

Pentecost

72

O Holy Spirit, Breath of God, blow in our lives this day.
clear out the cobwebs of closed minds and outworn ideas.
fill us with the freshness of your living love.
cleanse and renew us that we might go from this place
ready to be your people in the world.
we ask this in the name of the one who came
to reconcile the world to you, even Jesus Christ.

Pentecost

73

Spirit of God,
as a dove you come to us
with the offer of your peace,
creating order from chaos,
restoring the broken relationship between God and creation,
gently healing the wounds of divided humanity.

Spirit of God,
as fire you come to us,
setting the Church ablaze with your love,
consuming all that is unworthy,
strangely warming the hearts of your people
with new zeal.

Spirit of God,
as wind you come to us,
letting loose your power,
unseen,
unpredictable,
that changes the course of history.

Come, Spirit of God,
to us.

Pentecost

74

Lord God, we pray that as the Holy Spirit came in wind and fire to the apostles, so may he come to us, breathing new life into our lives, and setting our hearts aflame with love: through Jesus Christ our Lord.

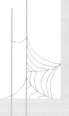

Trinity

Creator God, you spoke
and at your word the universe came into being,
drawn from the mass and mess of chaos,
and shaped to its beauty by your hand:
carving the rock and loosing the river.
We see your glory in the world around us.

Jesus, Word made flesh, you spoke
and at your word sins were forgiven,
broken lives were made whole,
troubled minds found peace,
and children and women and men
turned their lives in a new direction
to follow you.
We sense your presence with us
as your people gather in your name.

Holy Spirit, gentle as the dove,
wild as the wind, you spoke
and at your word the good news
of God's love in Jesus
ran round the globe.
We hear your voice in bible and preacher
and we come to worship you now.

To you, living God,
Creator, Saviour and life-giving Spirit
be praise and glory evermore.

Harvest

76

Generous God,
we look around today
and see ample evidence
of your goodness;
you have given us so much
and we are thankful.

We celebrate, too,
the unexpected harvests;
from questioning, a deeper faith
from despair, renewed hope
from estrangement, reconciliation
from guilt, acceptance
from loneliness, fellowship.

We trust you for the harvest
of seeds sown
which have yet to come to fruition.

To your name be praise and glory evermore.

All Saints

77

Saints
are not plastic and unreal,
with harps and halos.
They are ordinary folk
like you and me,
with problems and dreams.
yet in the way they respond to God's love
they are unique.
let us greet them all,
for they have created history.

We praise your name, God our King,
for your faithful people in all generations.

Thank you, God,
for the ordinary genuine folk
who have no pretensions of holiness,
no thought of future reward,
yet who declare your purpose and way
in thought, word and deed.

Thank you, God,
for the very special people
who proclaim your victory
even through the hardest suffering.
they never lose a grip on your love;
their faith and hope declare your glory.

· · · · ·

. . . . .

Thank you, God,
for those amazing Christians,
who are shining examples of unselfishness.
They never talk about themselves,
but listen intently to others.
They make everyone feel special and important,
they spread encouragement and joy.

Thank you, God,
for those who have shown immense courage,
when persecution and oppression have reigned;
for those who have suffered indignity and torture
rather than renounce the good news.
These people have brought the freedom we enjoy
and their lives declare your eternal victory.
We praise your name, God our King,
for your faithful people in all generations.

Christian Aid and One World Week

78

Creating God,
the earth is yours and all that is in it
the world and all who live in it.

This is your generous gift
help us to enjoy it.

This is our fragile trust
teach us to care for it.

This is your undeserved goodness
set us free to share it.

Christian Aid and One World Week

79

Compassionate God,
we thank you for teaching us
to care for our sisters and brothers
who live and die
along the margins of our world,
imprisoned in
poverty,
powerlessness,
prejudice........ .

But we stand now in your presence,
hesitant,
shifting our weight from one foot to the other,
knowing that we need to ask one thing more,
and counting the cost of asking;
yet we can do no other.

So give us, compassionate and passionate God,
the holy rage
which the prophets had
and Jesus had
which will take us beyond mercy
to strive for justice
in your broken and divided world.

Christian Unity

80

As we come together from the churches of this community
    may we know your presence, living God,

as we travel with one another in pilgrimage
    may we be open to new companions on the way

as we pray together
    may we discover the depths of unity in Christ

as we share our gifts with each other
    may we be ready to receive as well as to give

as we worship together
    may your Word come alive among us

as we laugh with one another
    may we see things from the perspective of joy

as we carry one another's burdens
    may we keep the law of Christ.

Church Anniversary

Prayers for looking ahead

81

God of the living past,
We thank you for the vision you gave
to those who built our church;
following their example,
help us to see
that we cannot live in the past, but that we must grow from it,
reaching out to today and tomorrow.

God of the exciting present,
help us to become the church
you want us to be now:
people of all ages
worshipping with joy,
sharing the good news of Jesus Christ,
serving with love,
learning the Christian way,
offering hope to all,
with no strings attached.

God of the beckoning future,
we wait for your surprises;
help us to hear your call
to take the risks of faith;
weave new patterns of ministry
from the gifts we offer.

Through Jesus Christ our Lord.

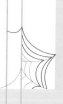

Vocations Sunday

82

Calling God,
we are surrounded by so many
discordant voices;
we are faced by so many
different choices.

Uncertain,
sometimes confused,
but believing you call
all of us
and each of us
to a unique ministry,
speak
and help us,
to hear again
however faintly,
your claim upon our lives:
'Follow me'.

Some Off-beat Prayers

Agenda for Today

83

1.   Warmly welcome any newcomers *and* the old-timers.

2.   Pray for comfort for those who are sad and guidance for those who are joyful.

3.   Pray for the young, old, black, white, male, female and all those who are somewhere in between.

4.   Offer a cuddle to someone who's lonely, or worried, and a soft shoulder to someone who's tired.

5.   Give a firm handshake to someone who's timid and share a good joke with an old friend – and even introduce the two!

6.   Congratulate someone who's had success this week and encourage someone who has failed to try again.

7.   Keep an eye out for anyone who's lost, bend an ear to somebody's problems and offer love from the heart.

8.   Give a compliment where it is due and sow seeds of confidence.

9.   Speak spiritually yet truthfully *and* be ready to *learn something new* about *God's* spirit and truth today.

10. Be sure to recognise myself in every person I meet.

God's Morning

84

Good morning – God's morning – O Lord my God!
I trust it will end with Good Night;
And in between I pray it will be a Good Day
As I try to be good, God, all-right (?!).

What I Will

85

Father, you gave me a mind so I could think and have
freedom of choice.
Don't let my thoughts go beyond my faith
lest I become dispassionate, cynical, self-loathing and
unbothered.

*I will my mind to be active so that I know what you need of
me and how to get on with it.*

Jesus, you gave me a heart so I could love and live for others.
Don't let my love be for evil or the distasteful
lest I become disappointed, jealous, lustful, greedy or selfish.

I will my heart to love goodness and seek it in all I encounter.

Holy Spirit, you gave me a soul so I could care and give of
myself through my life.
Don't let my soul be seized by bitterness and resentment
lest I become empowered in bringing down others around
me, stealing their happiness and innocence.

*I will my soul to reach out and touch people's lives with your
truth so that we can rejoice in it together.*

That is what I will, Lord.
Trusting it is your will too, I pray you will strengthen me
with your blessing – mind, heart and soul.

The Real Celebration

86

Christmas takes up half of the year ...
mostly at parties and shops
or drinking good health to our merry companions
or sitting alone wondering where the old days went
or spending a fortune on throw-away wrapping,
debates who we least want to see in the New Year with
till January Sales end and it stops.

Easter means chocolate and chickens
a movie repeat on TV,
another palm cross added to the collection,
and Agape supper though you've eaten already,
and furniture sales which must end on Good Friday
the smallest surprises in foil-wrapped temptations
and two minutes' prayer to a tree.

Harvest means shopping at Sainsburys
to gather the pasta shells in
and last-minute baskets of bruised fruit and ribbons
and memories of when the Church smelled of fresh baking
and *more fruit and flow'rs* than you **ever** smell *these days,*
the shiniest beauty, proud, straight from the orchard...
time-saving and pre-packed in tins.

. . . . .

With every year, as I grow older,
your parties, Lord, nothing but chores,
the same boring presents, the same tiresome troubles,
the same exclamations, the muttered expletives,
the hassle, the rushing, resentment, blurred motives,
debating, depression, fatigue, spending money,
same grating obsession, closed eyes, ears and doors.

(breathe…)

I reach, in despair, for your stillness, your quiet
your beauty, your freedom, your incense, your candles
your Word in the Bible, your hearing me praying,
palms upward, deep breaths…. grant me peace, Lord –
I'm Yours.

I See the Church

87

I see the Church as weak as me,
shirking responsibility.
It means to do things, but does not.
I think, "What a pathetic lot!"

I see the Church, cold as my heart,
A handshake and a world apart –
the martyred hymns, the prayer-time drone.
I think, "I'm best off on my own".

I see the Church and know my place;
my fate is set in time and space.
The Church will *never* change a thing.
I think, *"How very comforting!".*

I see the Church, my 9-to-6:
"Exec suite, nightclub in the crypt".
The locals rallied – now they shrug;
I think they've kicked their Sunday drug.

I see the Church, my home from home;
love thrives there, where my faith has grown.
I'll work till I can work no more
to save this house, his open door.

A Prayer for the Life of the Church

88

The Church began with your death, Lord –
the world was alive with your Word.
like wild fire, it burned in believers
and saved every sinner who heard!

They *would not* stop, they *had to shout*,
they took it in and I *let it out!*
And, free from chains, they travelled light –
they danced in prison every night,
gave heaven to those who gave them hell –
through love, they broke the devil's spell!

Two thousand years of love's glory,
a world filled with Love Divine,
The Church began with your death, Lord,
I *won't* let it end with mine.

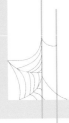

Prayer for the Start of Worship

89

Trust God to take care of everything while I'm sat in here
worshipping.
Typical.
The minute I turn my back from all those things I've got to
get done and start concentrating on something else.
*like giving thanks for my many blessings…or sharing Holy
Communion with my Church family, most of whom, I only get
to see and love once a week because I'm so busy,*
there he is, off, sorting everything out without me to
oversee or anything.
And after all that effort I've put in.
Peanuts to him!
Typical.
And the *really clever* thing is, he can listen to me *and*
answer my prayers *and* fill me with the Holy Spirit *at the
same time*!!
Amazing, that God.
Oh well.
Obviously, I'm not needed out there right now.
Might as well carry on with worshipping and that.
A job worth doing is worth doing well, so I'd best throw
my whole self into that instead. Probably get a lot more done
if I leave him to it, anyway.
Thank God for that.
A bit of peace…that's what I need.

Vestry Prayer

An address to the People of God before embarking on this morning's worship

90

Have you remembered to put the dinner in the oven?
Did you set the video recorder before you left?
Have you ironed your shirt for work?
Brought the washing in?
Let the cat out?
Reminded Grandad to take his medication?
Rung whatshername to wish her a happy birthday?
Packed for your holiday?
Vacuumed and dusted for your visitors this afternoon?
Dropped that note 'round to hoojah about this week's
meeting before he leaves?
Rung thingy to ask if he wants a lift?

No? Well, tough.
It's too late.
There's nothing you can do so why worry?
Forget it. Don't even think about fidgeting.
And for God's sake, don't sit there kicking yourself –
or anyone else for that matter!
You're in his hands now.
If it's really important, he'll deal with it.
trust.
Be grateful for small mercies…and much bigger ones.

God is my refuge and strength. A very present help in trouble.

Vestry Prayer

91

To build a good relationship with the Lord
We must set aside time for him each day.

How hard is that?

How many other things do we have to think about which
steal our thoughts away form our
one-way conversations?

166 hours of every week are spent on living.
2 hours per week are God-given time without breaking
the routine.

It is not a break from the norm to go to Church on Sunday.
2 hours only.
May we not stray from the point of today, wasting
our chances.

This is God-given time. Let us give it all – everything –
back to him with thanks.

Vestry Prayer

We are all here to worship the Lord God, Creator of all things…
So let's look forward to it!

We are here to celebrate and strengthen our relationship
with Jesus…
So let's make the most of this short time set aside in our
weekly routine.

We are all here to pray together as one living body,
the Church…
So let us fuel the fire in each other and be a true example
of directional purpose.

We are all here to say sorry for our failings…
In the knowledge of his forgiveness, let us not dwell on these
personal pressures – they waste
so much time which could be spent in positive mending.

Let us love God and one another, trust Jesus and welcome
the Holy Spirit into our service,
in the name of the Trinity who surrounds and protects us
and urges us forward.

Vestry Prayer

93

Take a moment to look around at the faces in this room.
...faces of those leading today's worship – the focal point of
this Church of Jesus Christ.

Jesus' peace and love for me must begin each one of
these faces...
...and must end with all the world united.

During our act of worship today, during each prayer and hymn,
let us listen to the voices that surround us –
voices of the people sharing in worship with us.

As I listen to the leader's words, as I say the Lord's prayer
and sing hymns of praise,
as I let my joy come from our being together – all for one
with each other –
each of those joyful, loving and pleading voices will be heard
by Jesus

Our life in him begins with the sharing

Let all I do today be in his name.

Good Friday Prayer of Confession

94

At this time of each year
we focus on one cross
on one man
on one event in history
with sadness and regret
at the behaviour of our predecessors.

How many millions of crosses
of men, women and children
of countless times over the ages and today
do we *not* stop to regret *for one minute* and *on our own behalf*?
Do we never give another thought to
not feel shocked and angry and sad about?
…Rejection, humiliation, loneliness, depression and despair…
how many crosses have we helped to build?
We have planted that first seed
or watered the roots
or chopped down the tree
or cut the wood
or fixed the pieces together
or set it high upon a hill for everyone to see
or drive the nails into hands and feet –
the last straw.

We are responsible for every thought, word and deed.
May love be the influence in all of these,
considerate of others' needs and what makes them tick…

· · · · ·

. . . . .

Each time we go to make a joke at their expense
may we make one about ourselves instead.
Each time we turn from their undesirable company
may we put our arms around them and invite them to our party.
Each time we open our mouths to curse their differences
may we look in their eyes and liken their needs to our own.

In the name of Our Lord, Jesus Christ –
a loving and vulnerable man
who died that no-one may ever die again...
live for Christ
live like Christ
love like Christ

Good Friday Prayer of Purpose

95

We will not fall asleep when darkness is upon us
just because we are tired of it all and want to shut our eyes
to our greatest fears.
We will be a watchful people.

We will not deny you; Lord, we know and love you.
We will not be afraid to love each other as brothers and sisters
in you.
We will be a proud people.

We will not jeer, laugh at you,
hate and fear you, vent our anger
we will be a compassionate people.

We have learned our lessons from the teachings of the
Easter story
we will act with hindsight always
look out for one another
stand up for one another
share our burdens and help one another off the crosses we bear,
cleanse each other's wounds,
love and keep one another, even if it makes us look foolish and the
jeering crowd is against
us.

If sadness and regret are not about doing better next time,
what are they?

We will live for Christ
we will live like Christ
we will love like Christ

Contributors Sources and Acknowledgements

Permission has been sought from all the copyright holders.

Common Order is published by St Andrew Press (1996); the extracts are used by permission of the Panel of Worship of the Church of Scotland
39, 64, 66;

The Revd Kate Compston is a minister of the United Reformed Church
16;

The Revd Geoffrey Dunstan is a minister of the United Reformed Church serving in Sussex
49;

Faith Burning Brightly is a collection of prayers written by members of Sutton Coldfield United Reformed Church, Gracechurch Centre. The prayers are used by permission
3, 22, 23, 28, 29, 30, 56, 63, 67, 69, 71, 73, 75, 80, 81;

The Revd Paul Floe is a minister of the United Reformed Church serving in Lincoln
14, 17;

For The Love of God, the Prayer Handbook 1996 published by the United Reformed Church
65, 70;

Rue-eth Fortey is a member of the United Reformed Church, now continuing her music studies in Boston USA
83, 84, 85, 86, 87, 88, 89, 90, 91, 92, 93, 94, 95;

Iona Community Worship Book © Wild Goose Publications, The Iona Community, Glasgow 1988, used by permission
19;

The Revd David Jenkins is a minister of the United Reformed Church serving in Wilmslow
32, 44, 57, 58, 68, 77;

The Revd A Ward Jones is Chair of the Bristol District of the Methodist Church. The prayer is taken from *All Things New* the prayer handbook of the Methodist Church 1999-2000;
46;

Barbara McDowell is an elder of the United Reformed Church
53, 76;

The Revd Kate McIlhagga is a minister of the United Reformed Church serving in the Northumberland District
43;

The Revd Peter McIntosh is a minister of the United Reformed Church serving as Director of the Windermere Centre and Moderator of the General Assembly 1999-2000
24;

The Revd Barbara Meachin is a minister of the United Reformed Church now retired. These prayers are from her book Opening Words, Prayers and Poems for Worship © 1996 Barbara Meachin; used by permission
34, 37;

Jenny Mills is a member of the United Reformed Church
18;

Jane Nash is an elder of the United Reformed Church
21;

The Revd Bar Nash-Williams is an Anglican priest serving in the parish of Tettenhall Wood, Wolverhampton in the Diocese of Lichfield
2, 5, 6, 7, 8, 9, 10, 11, 13;

The Revd Hugh Neems is a minister of the United Reformed Church now retired
1;

The Revd David Owen is a minister of the United Reformed Church now retired
25;

Patterns and Prayers for Christian Worship
Published by Oxford University Press for the Baptist Union (1991); used by permission
61;

Prayers for Use in Church
© Jack Masterton 1993; published by St Andrew Press, used by permission
15, 74;

Susan Sayers is the author of numerous books for use in worship. Used by permission from *To Worship in Stillness* © Kevin Mayhew Ltd, Licence Number 005032
27;

The Revd John Slow is a minister of the United Reformed Church now retired
4, 20, 40, 41, 45, 51, 52, 55, 60, 78, 79, 82;

Scottish Liturgy 1982 published by the General Synod of the Scottish Episcopal Church
54, 62;

Unifying Assembly of the Congregational Union of Scotland and the United Reformed Church in the United Kingdom Order of Worship 2000
31, 42, 50;

United Churches of Christ Worship Book published by the United Churches of Christ; used by permission
12, 72;

The Revd Elizabeth Welch is the Moderator of the West Midlands Province of the United Reformed Church
35, 36;

The Revd Peter Whittaker is Chair of the West Yorkshire District of the Methodist Church. The prayer is taken from *All Things New* the prayer handbook of the Methodist Church 1999-2000;
48;

Sheila Williams is an elder of the United Reformed Church
59;

World Council of Churches
47.

Numerical Index

1	Hugh Neems
2	Bar Nash-Williams
3	Faith Burning Brightly
4	John Slow
5	Bar Nash-Williams
6	Bar Nash-Williams
7	Bar Nash-Williams
8	Bar Nash-Williams
9	Bar Nash-Williams
10	Bar Nash-Williams
11	Bar Nash-Williams
12	United Churches of Christ Worship Book
13	Bar Nash-Williams
14	Paul Floe
15	Jack Masterton in Prayers for Use in Church
16	Kate Compston
17	Paul Floe
18	Jenny Mills
19	Iona Community Worship Book
20	John Slow
21	Jane Nash
22	Faith Burning Brightly
23	Faith Burning Brightly
24	Peter McIntosh, Day of Prayer for the General Assembly 1999
25	David Owen
26	Source untraced
27	Susan Sayers
28	Faith Burning Brightly
29	Faith Burning Brightly
30	Faith Burning Brightly
31	Unifying Assembly Order of Worship
32	David Jenkins
33	Prayer Handbook
34	Barbara Meachin
35	Elizabeth Welch
36	Elizabeth Welch
37	Barbara Meachin
38	Source untraced
39	Common Order